God comes to us like a caterpillar:

Jesus' stories retold for kids

For the Shelton - Jenk's

Kent Chadwick

all blessings,

Kit Chadwick

Wisdom

Press

Wisdom Press

Bainbridge Island & Pebble Beach

6922 Baker Hill Rd. NE
Bainbridge Island, WA 98110

www.WisdomPress.org
wisdompress@mindspring.com

Library of Congress Cataloguing-in-Publication Data
Chadwick, Kent, 1955-. God comes to us like a caterpillar:
Jesus' stories retold for kids.
Summary: A retelling of all 78 of Jesus' stories using
examples from kids' lives today.
Jesus Christ—Parables—Juvenile literature; Bible stories,
English—N.T.; Parables. Index.
ISBN 1452889228
EAN-13 9781452889221

Cover photo used with permission from Jupiterimages

Caterpillar line drawing used with permission from Pearson
S. Foresman and M. De Kievith

For Ali

Table of Contents

Introduction

The stories Jesus told are the wisest stories I know. They are sometimes smart and sometimes simple, sometimes funny and sometimes sad, sometimes familiar and sometimes strange. Yet all of them are little answers to big mysteries.

Jesus was a teacher, a Jewish rabbi, who walked from village to village teaching the people that God was coming to them.

"How will God come to us?" the people wanted to know.

So Jesus told stories to tell them how God comes to us.

"If God is coming to us, then what should we do? How should we behave?" the people wanted to know.

So Jesus told stories about what we should do.

"Who is this Jesus who says he knows about God?" the people wanted to know.

So Jesus told them stories about who he was.

Jesus didn't speak English. In fact, when Jesus was teaching in Israel 2,000 years ago, the English language didn't even exist. Jesus spoke Aramaic and Hebrew, and maybe even

Introduction

Greek. His friends remembered the stories he told and then told them to other people all around the Mediterranean Sea. Eventually those stories were written down in Greek in the Bible gospels of Matthew, Mark, Luke, and John. "Gospel" means a good tale, a good tale about Jesus.

The Greek gospels have been translated into languages all over the world, including English.

So Jesus' stories are old. He told them to adults. He spoke in ancient languages. He used examples from people's lives 2,000 years ago when many people spent their time herding sheep, taking care of olive trees, or fishing with nets.

I think it's hard for American children to understand and enjoy these wise old stories. So in this book I've tried to retell Jesus' stories using examples from our life today in the 21st century. I've read each story and thought about the mystery it presents. I've tried to understand how the story answers that mystery. Then I've tried to think of an example from your everyday life as an American kid that would also give you a bit of that same answer. These are the retellings I came up with. I pray that some are close to the answers

Introduction

Jesus gave to the big mysteries he taught about.

I start most of the stories with the words "Jesus said," but that isn't true of course. He didn't use these words; he didn't tell the stories this way. I write "Jesus said" at the beginning of these stories for one reason only—to surprise you. The stories Jesus told almost always surprised the people listening. I think that if you're surprised by these stories it will be easier for you to find the answers Jesus gave us so many years ago. After each story I ask some questions, which may help you think more about the meaning of that story for you and your life.

Whether or not you like my retellings, be sure to take a careful look at Jesus' stories in the gospels when you're ready. Those are the stories to really pay attention to. To help you find them I've noted down at the end of each story where you can find the original story in the Bible. For example, the note "Matthew 13:31-32" tells you to look at verses 31 to 32 in the 13th chapter of the gospel of Matthew. Many of Jesus' stories appear in more than one of the gospels, so I've listed all the places where you can find versions of the same story. After you read Jesus' stories in the gospels you might even want to retell some of them

Introduction

yourself. I would enjoy reading your retellings if you would like to email them to me at: wisdompress@mindspring.com.

Enjoy!

Kent Chadwick
Bainbridge Island,
Washington

How Does God Come To Us?

Jesus said, "One day a rich woman planned a treasure hunt for four kids in the neighborhood. She gave each of them a treasure map. One of the kids couldn't read, so he dropped the map and went off to play. The second kid could read, so she got excited because the map said there was a buried treasure hidden somewhere. She followed the map until she came to a nearby forest; but the forest scared her and she ran back home. The third kid followed the map all the way through the forest. But after that he got bored, and went and opened a lemonade stand instead. The fourth kid, however, followed the map carefully to the end, and there she found a box full of silver dollars."

"The parable of the sower,"
Matthew 13:3-8; Mark 4:3-8; Luke 8:4-8

How Does God Come To Us?

What happens when God comes to you? Why do some people get it and some people don't?

2

How Does God Come To Us?

Jesus said, "God comes to us like when Jack's mother threw the magic beans out the window. She thought they were worthless. Yet while they slept the great beanstalk grew. When they woke up they couldn't understand how that beanstalk had appeared. But Jack knew that the beanstalk was there for him to climb. So he did climb, and what did he find? Great treasure."

"The parable of the seed cast on the earth," Mark 4:26-29

Has God ever come to you in a little way that turned out to be big?

3

How Does God Come To Us?

Jesus said, "God comes to us like a man who leaves a large bowl of candy out on his porch on Halloween. Later that night he hears a knock and opens his front door. There are some children at the door who look upset.

"'Why is there junk in your candy bowl?' they ask.

"The man looks in and sees pieces of chewed bubble gum and half-eaten lollipops in the bowl.

"'Some joker has tried to spoil my candy bowl,' the man says.

"'Will you throw it all away?' the children ask.

"'No,' the man says, 'It's too dark to see and I don't want to throw away the good candy with the bad. Come back tomorrow morning and I'll bring out a table. We will spread the candy out, and sort the good into one pile and the bad into another. Then I'll throw the bad out into the garbage. But the good candy I'll give to you, and you can share it among yourselves and with your friends.'"

"The parable of the wheat and tares," Matthew 13:24-30

How Does God Come To Us?

Have you ever felt like asking God, "Hey, why is there junk in your candy bowl?" What was that feeling?

How Does God Come To Us?

    "I tell you the truth," Jesus said, "unless you are changed like Cinderella was changed God can't come to you."

"The allegory of being born of the spirit," John 3:3-8

Have you ever felt changed in a big way? What was it like? Did God come to you?

How Does God Come To Us?

One person asked Jesus, "Will only a few people get to go to God's house?"

Jesus answered, "God's house is on a side street. All the people going down the main streets will miss it. Go down the side street. And the door to God's house is skinny. You have to squeeze through it. Keep squeezing."

"The proverb of the narrow door,"
Matthew 7:13-14; Luke 13:23-24

Have you found God's house yet?

How Does God Come To Us?

Jesus said, "When the play has started and the theater owner closes the doors and you come late and say, 'Let us in.'

"She'll say, 'I don't know you.'

"Then you'll say, 'But we come to plays here all the time.'

"And still she'll answer, 'Go away, I don't remember you.'"

"The parable of the housemaster shutting the door," Luke 13:25-27

Have you ever been late with God?

How Does God Come To Us?

Jesus said, "People from India to Israel, from Scandinavia to South Africa, will sit down together when God comes to us.

"Look and see: some who were last will be first, and some who were first will be last."

"The proverb of the last that shall be first," Luke 13:28-30

Have you ever been moved from the back to the front of a line? How did you feel?

How Does God Come To Us?

"How should I describe people who complain about how God comes to us?" Jesus asked. "What are they like? They are like kids who sneer at other kids on the playground and yell, 'You didn't dance when we said dance. You didn't cry when we said cry.'"

"The parable of children sitting in the marketplace," Luke 7:31-35

Have you ever tried to tell God what to do? Why?

How Does God Come To Us?

Jesus said, "God won't come to someone who starts the race but then looks back at other things."

"The proverb of the hand to the plough," Luke 9:62

Have you ever looked at God and felt everything else disappear? What was that feeling like?

How Does God Come To Us?

Jesus looked at all the people following him and loved them. He turned to his friends and said, "God's restaurant is full of people, but there aren't enough waitresses and waiters. Pray that God hires more waiters and waitresses right away."

"The allegory of the plentiful harvest," Matthew 9:37-38; Luke 10:2

Has God ever sent you to help someone? When?

How Does God Come To Us?

Jesus said, "God comes to us like a caterpillar. It's hard to notice a caterpillar. It's little and ugly and stuck on a tree. But one day the caterpillar changes. The caterpillar becomes ... a moth. And that moth flies everywhere, beautifully."

"The parable of the grain of mustard seed," Matthew 13:31-32; Mark 4:30-32; Luke 13:18-19

Has God ever come to you and you didn't even notice? When?

How Does God Come To Us?

Jesus said, "God comes to us like a joke that one girl tells another in the back of the room. Soon the joke spreads through the whole class and makes everyone laugh."

"The parable of the leaven,"
Matthew 13:33; Luke 13:20-21

Have you ever seen God spread from person to person? When?

How Does God Come To Us?

Jesus said, "God comes to us like a girl who finds a beautiful old doll in an abandoned tree house. Right away she goes to the family who built the tree house years before and gets permission to make the tree house hers."

"The parable of the treasure in the field," Matthew 13:44

Have you ever found one of God's treasures? What did you do?

How Does God Come To Us?

Jesus said, "God comes to us like a boy at a garage sale who finds the baseball card he's always wanted. He rushes home, gets all the money he's saved, and runs back to buy it."

"The parable of the pearl of great price," Matthew 13:45-46

When have you given up something so that God would come to you?

How Does God Come To Us?

Jesus said, "God comes to us like a girl who goes fishing. The big fish that she catches she keeps to take home. But the little ones she throws back into the river."

"The parable of the net cast into the sea," Matthew 13:47-50

Have you ever felt God catch you? What happened?

How Does God Come To Us?

Jesus said, "Every well-behaved kid who learns how God comes to us is like a cook who can learn new recipes as well as follow the old ones."

"The proverb of the scribe who becomes a disciple," Matthew 13:52

What are the old ways that God comes to us? What are the new ways?

How Does God Come To Us?

"What do you think?" Jesus asked, "If a girl has six kittens and one of them wanders off in the neighborhood, won't she leave the other five and go looking for the one that's lost? Won't she wander through the streets? And if she finds it won't she be happier with that kitten than with the other five that stayed safe? She will call her friends and say, 'Let's have a party; I found my lost kitten!' The same is true with your Father in heaven who doesn't want any little one to be lost."

"The parable of the lost sheep,"
Matthew 18:12-14; Luke 15:3-7

Have you ever felt lost from God? When?

How Does God Come To Us?

Jesus said, "God comes to us like a mother who comes home and sits down to find out what her children have been doing while she's been gone. Her son, it seems, has broken a very expensive vase because he was kicking a ball around the living room.

"'You're going to have to pay for that vase out of your allowance and your savings,' the mother says.

"'But Mom,' the boy says, 'I'm sorry. I've been saving for the bike I want and I've almost got enough. If I have to pay you back, I won't get the bike for another year. Please. I won't do it again.'

"'Alright,' the mother says, 'I forgive you. I won't make you pay for it.'

"But then that son goes into his room and finds his little sister playing with his remote control car. She isn't supposed to be his room, so she gets scared and drops the controls on the floor. It cracks in two.

"'You broke it,' the brother yells, 'you have to buy me a new one.'

"'But, I can't,' his sister cries, 'This costs a lot. I don't have a lot of money.'

"'We'll see about that,' the brother says, and he drags his sister into her room, makes her empty her piggy banks, and takes every penny she has.

"Their older sister, who sees this, gets angry, and she tells their mother what their brother has done.

"Then the mother calls her son into the living room. 'I am so mad at you. Didn't I forgive you for breaking the vase when you begged me? Couldn't you have forgiven your sister when she broke your toy? But since you grabbed every penny from your sister, I will grab every penny from you. I'm going to take your savings, and your allowance too, until you've paid for that entire vase.'"

"The parable of the pitiless slave," Matthew 18:23-35

Who has forgiven you something? Who haven't you forgiven yet?

How Does God Come To Us?

The people brought their children to Jesus so he could touch them and pray over them. His friends didn't like this and they shooed the children away.

But Jesus said, "Stop. Let the children come to me. God comes to children."

To the adults he said, "You must become a child again if you want God to come to you."

Then Jesus put his hands on the children and blessed them.

"The proverb of the children," Matthew 18:2-4; Matthew 19:13-15; Mark 10:13-16; Luke 18:15-17

What can kids teach grownups about how God comes to us?

How Does God Come To Us?

Jesus said, "It is easier for a horse to go through a shoe lace hole than for God to come to someone who's rich."

"Then whom can God come to?" asked Jesus' friends.

"What's impossible for people is possible for God," Jesus answered.

"The proverb of the camel through the eye of the needle," Matthew 19:23-26; Mark 10:23-27; Luke 18:24-27

What's the problem with being rich?

How Does God Come To Us?

Jesus said, "God comes to us like a man who goes outside very early on a Saturday and hires neighborhood children to work in his yard. He agrees to pay each of them $50 for a day's work and sends them to cut his lawn, rake his leaves, and weed his garden. At 10 a.m. he goes out again and sees children playing on the street and asks them if they'd like to work today.

"'Go and work in my yard and I'll pay you what is right,' the man tells the children and they go to work.

"In the afternoon at both 1 and 4 p.m. the man does the same thing. Then about 6 p.m. the man goes out in the neighborhood and sees some other children just hanging out. 'Don't you want to earn some money today?' he asks.

"'Sure,' they say, 'but nobody's asked us.'

"'All of you go into my yard where the others are working and help, and I'll pay you what is right,' the man says.

"At 7 p.m. he tells all the children to stop work and come over to him. He pays each of them, beginning with those who started to work last. To those who started at 6 p.m. he gives $50. So when he gets to those who started very early in the morning, they think they'll get much more. But the man gives each of them $50 too, and they get mad.

"'Those kids only worked one hour and you gave them the same as us. But we worked for eleven hours, even when it was hot outside.'

"'My children,' the man says, 'I haven't wronged you. I paid you what I promised. You agreed to work for that much. Take your money and go on home. I've paid the same to the last children and to you. Can't I give my money as I please? Is my goodness making you greedy?'"

"The parable of the generous lord of the vineyard," Matthew 20:1-16

Does God ever seem too nice? When?

Jesus said, "God comes to us like the president who threw a birthday party for his daughter. He invited all of the children in her class. But on the day of the party they didn't come. So the president sent his aides to go and bring them to the party.

"The aides went and said, 'The birthday party is ready. A great room has been decorated. The games are planned. The prizes are wrapped. A beautiful birthday cake is baked. Come to the party.' But the classmates laughed at the aides, and went off to play soccer or to go to the mall. Some of the kids even broke the windows in the aides' cars.

"When the president heard about this he was furious and called the police who arrested the kids who had broken the windows. Then he said to his aides, 'The children who were invited weren't respectful. Go instead to all of the children around the neighborhood here and invite them to the party.'

"So the aides went down the streets and into the apartment houses all around. They invited all the children they found, both well-behaved and rowdy kids. The kids got dressed for the party and came and filled up the great room.

"When the president came in to meet all the children, he saw one girl who hadn't gotten dressed for the party. The president asked her, 'Dear, why did you come without getting dressed for the party?' The girl couldn't say anything. The president said to his aides, 'She can't stay for the fun. Take her home.'"

"The parable of the prince's marriage," Matthew 22:1-14

When did you accept an invitation from God? When did you refuse one?

27

How Does God Come To Us?

Jesus said, "Happy are the children who are watching their younger sisters or brothers when their parents come home. Their parents will be pleased and will sit them down for a special treat. And if their parents come home two hours late, or three hours late and find them carefully watching their sisters and brothers, happy are those children.

"Watch because you don't know when God will come to you. If the student knew when the teacher was going to give the pop quiz he would study and be ready and do well on the test.

"Be ready, because God comes to you when you least expect it."

"The parable of the watching servants," Mark 13:34-36; Luke 12:35-38
"The parable of the housemaster knowing the hour of the thief," Matthew 24:42-44; Luke 12:39-40

When has God come to you when you weren't expecting?

How Does God Come To Us?

Jesus told the people who followed him this story, "There was a father who came into the living room of his house and stepped in a mess his son's puppy had left on the floor.

"The father got angry and yelled at his son, 'You've had this puppy for six months and it's not house-trained yet? We're going to get rid of this dog.'

"But the son answered, 'Give me two more months, Dad. I'll keep walking her and training her, and she should be house trained soon. But if she isn't, then we'll get rid of her. O.K.?'"

"The parable of the fig tree without fruit," Luke 13:6-9

When has God given you a second chance?

How Does God Come To Us?

    "Be ready," Jesus said, "God comes to us when we don't expect it. Who's the clever kid when the teacher has to go to the office? It's the kid who's helping the class behave when the teacher returns. The teacher will give that kid important jobs to do. But the foolish kid thinks, 'The teacher's not coming back for awhile,' and begins to tease the other students and throw things around the class. That kid's teacher will come back when she doesn't expect it and punish her for acting up."

"The parable of the wise and evil servants," Matthew 24:45-51; Luke 12:42-48

When has God caught you doing something good? When has God surprised you when you were doing something wrong?

How Does God Come To Us?

Jesus' friends asked him, "When will God come in power to save us?"

Jesus said, "Many terrible things will happen; but that is not the time. Many people will come and say 'I am the Chosen One,' or 'The Chosen One is here, come and see.' Don't believe them. When God's Chosen One comes in power everyone will know. Learn the lesson of the dawn. When you see the first light in the east you know that morning has come."

"The parable of the fig tree's tender branches," Matthew 24:32-33; Mark 13:28-29; Luke 21:30-31

What do you hope will happen when God comes in power?

How Does God Come To Us?

One of the girls listening to Jesus said, "The kid who God comes to will sure be happy!"

And Jesus answered, "There was a boy who planned a big birthday party, and invited all of his friends. When everything was ready the boy's mom went to pick up the kids for the party. But all of them made excuses for why they couldn't come.

"The first one said, 'I've just bought a toy and I have to play with it now. Please excuse me.'

"Another one said, 'I've just bought a book and I have to see if I like it. Please excuse me.'

"And another one said, 'I've just made a new friend, so I can't come.'

"The boy's mom came back with an empty car and told him what had happened. The boy was angry. He said, 'Come on; let's go get some other kids from my class.' And the boy and his mom went and found kids who weren't his friends or who were unpopular or different and brought them to his house for the party.

"But there was still room for more, so the boy told his mom, 'Let's go outside and grab

How Does God Come To Us?

any kid coming by and make him come to the party so the room is full. I'm sure not going to let the kids I invited first eat any of my birthday cake.'"

"The parable of the great supper," Luke 14:15-24

When have you made an excuse to not join in on something God had planned for you? When have you been surprised to find God's included you in something?

How Does God Come To Us?

Jesus said, "If a girl has ten dollars yet loses one in her room, won't she turn on all her lights and clean her whole room and hunt for it until she finds it? And when she finds it she'll call to her brothers and sisters and mother and father and say, 'Hey, isn't it great? I found the dollar I lost!'"

"The parable of the lost drachma," Luke 15:8-10

When have you felt that God was searching for you?

How Does God Come To Us?

Jesus said, "One day a mother took her two daughters to an amusement park. But after she'd bought the tickets and they'd entered the gate, the youngest daughter said, 'Give me my tickets and I'm going to go and play by myself.'

"The mother divided up the tickets and gave the daughter her share. Then that youngest daughter ran off, laughing. She raced around the amusement park and used up her tickets quickly, doing whatever she wanted to do. But by noon she didn't have any tickets left. She didn't have any money for lunch either. She sat down on a bench, feeling hungry and bored.

"One of the amusement park attendants came by and said, 'Hey, if you don't have anything to do, clean up those picnic tables over there and I'll give you a ticket for the Ferris wheel.' So the girl started cleaning the picnic tables. It was hard work and she got hungrier and she even thought about eating some of the leftover food on the tables. Halfway through cleaning the picnic tables she sat down and cried.

"But she came to herself and remembered how her mother would always feed any neighborhood kid who came by their house, and here she was missing lunch. So she said to herself, 'I'll go and find Mother and tell her I was wrong, that I've ruined her day, and that I don't deserve anything more. And I'll ask her to just treat me for the rest of the day like a neighborhood kid who she happened to run into.' Then the girl got up and went looking for her mother.

"Now the mother spotted her youngest daughter from far away and was filled with love for her. She ran to her daughter, hugged her, and kissed her.

"Her daughter said, 'Mother, I was wrong. I've ruined your day and don't deserve anything more.'

"But the mother said, 'Quick, you need something special,' and she took her daughter over to a souvenir shop and bought her a pretty hat and a ring. Then she went over to the best restaurant in the amusement park and asked for a table, telling the hostess, 'My daughter ran away, but now she's back and we're going to celebrate.'

"Now when the oldest daughter saw all this, she got angry and wouldn't go into the restaurant. So the mother went out to talk with her. The oldest daughter said, 'I did everything you wanted me to do today, but you didn't buy me a hat or a ring. But when she comes back, having run off and fooled around all day, you take her to the best restaurant?'

"Then the mother said to her oldest daughter, 'Dear, you were with me all day today and everything I did you did too. Still, it's right for us to celebrate, because your sister ran away and now she's come back. She was lost, but now she is found.'"

"The parable of the prodigal son,"
Luke 15:11-32

When have you run away from God? When have you ever been jealous of someone who had been bad and still received something good from God?

How Does God Come To Us?

Jesus told this story, "At a certain school there was a principal who didn't care about God or about kids. And there was a boy who would come to the principal every day complaining about the bully who was bothering him. For a number of days the principal didn't do anything about the bully. But after awhile the principal said to herself, 'I don't care about God or about kids. However, since this boy keeps complaining, I'll punish the bully so that this boy stops bothering me.'

"Listen to what the bad principal said. Won't God come to the children who are crying for help night and day? I say God will come to them quickly."

"The parable of the judge who didn't fear God," Luke 18:1-8

When have you prayed and prayed for help? What happened?

How Does God Come To Us?

Jesus said, "God comes to us like two flower girls who took their baskets of freshly cut flowers and waited outside for the wedding to start. But the wedding didn't start because the bridegroom was late. Now one of the girls was clever and the other one was foolish. The sun was very hot that afternoon, so the clever flower girl went and got a bowl of water and arranged her flowers in the bowl to keep them fresh. The foolish flower girl left her flowers in the basket in the sun. Since the bridegroom still hadn't come both girls took a nap.

"All of a sudden there was a shout, 'The bridegroom is coming, get ready to start the wedding,' and both girls woke up and rushed to get their baskets. But the foolish girl found that her flowers were all wilted. She went to the clever girl, whose flowers still were fresh, and said, 'My flowers are all wilted. I can't use them. Please give me some of yours.' But the clever flower girl answered, 'No, there aren't enough to fill both baskets. Go down to the basement where they prepared the flowers and get some more for yourself.'

"So the foolish flower girl went downstairs to get some new flowers. But while she was gone the wedding music started and the clever flower girl led the way for the bride. When the foolish flower girl got back she found that the door was closed. She knocked on the door and said, 'Please let me in.' But a voice answered, 'Who are you? Go away, the wedding has started.'"

"The parable of the wise and foolish virgins," Matthew 25:1-13

What do you do to be ready for God to come to you?

Jesus said, "God comes to us like a teacher who asked her class to raise money for a special project. She gave each of her students an amount of money based on what she thought they could handle. She gave one student five dollars, another student two dollars, and another student one dollar. The teacher told them, 'Use this money to raise more money for our project over the vacation.'

"During the vacation the student who received the five dollars bought flour and sugar and chocolate chips, baked dozens of cookies, sold them to his neighbors, and made ten dollars. The student who had received the two dollars bought lemons and sugar and cups, opened a lemonade stand in the park, sold drinks to her friends, and made four dollars. But the student who had received one dollar was afraid of losing it and put it in her desk drawer.

"When the vacation was over and the students came back to class, the teacher had a student draw a chart on the board to write down how much money each student had raised. The student who had received the five dollars came up to the teacher and gave her the five dollars and five more.

"'Well done,' the teacher said, 'You did well with a little responsibility, now I'll give you a lot—you will be in charge of our next project. Come into the next room for our party.'

"The student who had received the two dollars came up to the teacher and gave her the two dollars and two more.

"'Good work,' the teacher said, 'You did well with a little responsibility, now I'll give you a lot—you'll be second in charge of our next project. Come into the next room for our party.'

"Then the student who had received the one dollar came up and gave the teacher the one dollar and said, 'I knew that you were stingy about money, that you didn't want to lose any, but expected that we'd make money for your project. So I was afraid to lose your dollar and I kept it in my desk drawer at home. Here it is.'

"The teacher got angry and said, 'You've failed this project. You knew I was stingy about money, and that I didn't want to lose any, and even expected you to make more, so you should at least have given your dollar to one of your classmates so that she could've used it and made more with it. But since you did nothing you won't be included in our next project and you can't come to the party.'

"Then the teacher said to the student writing the amounts on the board, 'Take that one dollar off from her name and add it to the total of the student who received the five dollars. Everyone who has a lot will get even more, but the person who has nothing will lose everything.'"

"The parable of the talents,"
Matthew 25:14-30; Luke 19:11-27

Have you ever used a gift God gave you? What happened?

What Do We Do?

Jesus said, "You are the light of the world. The bright lights of a city can't be hidden. No one lights the candles of a menorah and then puts it under the couch. Instead you put the menorah on a table so that it lights up the whole house. Let your light shine. Let everyone see the good things you do and they will praise God."

"The proverb of the lamp under the bushel," Matthew 5:14-16; Mark 4:21-22; Luke 8:16; Luke 11:33

What good things do you love to do?

What Do We Do?

Jesus said, "Why do you notice the speck of dust in your brother's eye and not see the wad of mud in your own? How can you say, 'Brother, let me take that speck out of your eye,' when you don't see the wad of mud in your own eye? You're talking the talk, but not walking the walk. First take the mud out of your own eye, and then you'll see clearly enough to help take the speck out of your brother's eye."

"The proverb of the mote in your brother's eye, the beam in your own," Matthew 7:3-5; Luke 6:41-42

When have you made fun of someone who did something that you do too?

What Do We Do?

Jesus said, "Watch out for evil adults who pretend to be sheep, but who really are wolves in sheep's clothing. You will know them by what they do.

"Do you find oranges in cigarette machines? Do you pick apples from parking meters?

"You don't get sour milk from a carton of good milk. You don't get good milk from a carton of sour milk. A good milk carton has only good milk for you to drink. A sour milk carton has only sour milk, and it will be thrown away.

"The good person does good things with the good in his heart. The evil person does evil things with the evil in his heart. What is in someone's heart comes out of his mouth."

"The proverb of wolves in sheep's clothing," Matthew 7:15
"The proverb of the good tree and the bad," Matthew 7:16-20; Luke 6:43-44
"The proverb of the treasure of the heart," Luke 6:45

How do you know when to trust an adult?

47

What Do We Do?

Jesus said, "The eye is your body's camera. If your eye is open, then your body will shine with light. But if your eye is closed, then your body will be dark. And if the camera inside you is dark, think how blank your film will be."

"The allegory of the eye as the lamp of the body," Matthew 6:22-23; Luke 11:34-36

What do you do to find out what's true?

What Do We Do?

Jesus said, "Ask for what you need and God will give it to you. If your dog were hungry would you give it rocks to eat? If your cat were thirsty would you give it hot sauce to drink? So, if as children you know how to give good gifts, how much more will God, your Father in heaven, give you the good things you ask for?"

"The parable of the son asking for bread," Matthew 7:9-11; Luke 11:11-13

When have you gotten what you prayed for? When haven't you?

What Do We Do?

Jesus said, "The child who hears what I say and does the things I tell her is like the clever little pig who built his house of bricks. When the wolf blew and blew, the house stood firm and the pig was safe. But the child who hears what I say and doesn't do the things I tell her is like the foolish little pig who built his house of straw. When the wolf blew and blew, his house fell down and he had to run for his life."

"The parable of building on rock or sand," Matthew 7:24-27; Luke 6:47-49

What have you done that Jesus told you to do?

What Do We Do?

"What do you think?" Jesus asked. "There were two students who both had to stay after school with the principal. One student's detention was for ten minutes and the other student's detention was for two hours. But since it was a fine day and each had a basketball game to play, the principal decided to forgive both of their detentions. So which of the students will love the principal more?"

"The parable of a certain creditor," Luke 7:40-43

Which of the students will love the principal more? Has God forgiven you a lot or a little?

What Do We Do?

Jesus said, "If playing with a toy makes you greedy, give that toy away. It's better not to have any toys than to be greedy. If playing a game makes you cheat, stop playing. It's better not to play games at all than to cheat. For every child will have growing pains."

"The proverb of the hand that offends," Matthew 18:8-9; Mark 9:43-48
"The proverb of being salted with fire," Mark 9:49

What's one of your growing pains?

What Do We Do?

Jesus said, "You are bubbly soda pop. But when the bubbles are gone the soda goes flat and it can't get its bubbles back again. What's the soda good for then? Keep your bubbles."

"The parable of salt," Matthew 5:13; Mark 9:50; Luke 14:34-35

What do people love about you?

What Do We Do?

Jesus said, "Do what you know is right. Make friends with the shop owner who's caught you stealing before he calls the police and they take you to the judge who puts you in juvenile hall. I tell you, you won't get out until you've done all your community service."

"The parable of going before the judge," Matthew 5:25-26; Luke 12:58-59

When have you made up with someone you hurt? When have you made up with God?

What Do We Do?

"I'm supposed to love my neighbor, but who is my neighbor?" asked a smart aleck, who was trying to make himself look good.

Jesus said, "A boy was walking from school downtown one afternoon when he was attacked by a gang of kids. They hit him, pushed him down and kicked him. They stole his backpack and even his sneakers and they left him lying on the sidewalk.

"It so happened that a Boy Scout was walking down the same street, but when he saw the boy lying on the sidewalk, he crossed over to the other side of the street and walked by.

"Now a Girl Scout came by. But she crossed to the other side of the street and ignored him, just like the Boy Scout.

"Then along came a big girl smoking a cigarette. When she saw the boy who was hurt, she stopped and reached down to help him. She wiped off the dirt and blood from his face with her t-shirt. She picked him up and carried him to a corner store. There she bought him a drink and told the clerk at the store to give the boy whatever he needed. 'I'll pay you back later. I have to go and tell his parents to come and take him home,' she said.

What Do We Do?

"So, which of these three kids acted like a neighbor to the boy who was hurt by the gang?"

"The one who was kind to him," answered the smart aleck.

"Go and do the same," Jesus told him.

"The parable of the good Samaritan," Luke 10:25-37

When have you acted like a neighbor? When haven't you?

What Do We Do?

Jesus said, "What if a friend of yours knocks on your door late at night and says, 'Hey, can I borrow your basketball? My cousin's come by and we want to play out on the lighted court and my ball's flat.'

"And you shout back from the living room, 'I'm watching T.V. don't bother me now, it's late. I don't want to try and find my basketball.'

"But I tell you, you'll get up and find the basketball and let him borrow it, maybe not because he's your friend, but because he keeps knocking and asking.

"So I say: ask and it will be given to you, look and you will find, knock and it will be opened for you."

"The parable of the friend at midnight," Luke 11:5-8

What have you been asking and asking God?

57

What Do We Do?

Jesus said, "A bully who is chased away wanders the streets and doesn't find any place to hang out. So he says, 'I'll go back to my old playground.' And when he returns he finds it empty, swept, and clean. He then goes and gets seven of his friends, who are even meaner than he is, to come hang out in that playground. Now that playground is worse than it was at first."

"The parable of the return of the unclean spirit," Matthew 12:43-45; Luke 11:24-26

When have you been bad and gotten worse? What happened?

What Do We Do?

Jesus said, "Don't get greedy; life isn't about how much you have." Then he told them a story, "There was a girl who had done a lot of babysitting all during the school year and had earned a lot of money. When school ended she took that money and bought herself two cases of chocolate bars to enjoy for the whole summer. And she went to hide those candy bars in the cabinet of her tree house. But the cabinet wasn't big enough to fit the boxes of chocolate, so she tore out the cabinet and spent a whole weekend building a bigger one to store her chocolate in.

"When she was done, she rubbed her stomach and said, 'Stomach, think of all the chocolate you'll be eating all summer long, just relaxing in my tree house.'

"But God said to her, 'Silly girl, tomorrow your stomach will be on a plane far away from here, because your parents are taking you on a surprise vacation for the whole summer. And the other kids in the neighborhood will be the ones who end up enjoying all your candy bars while you're gone.'"

"The parable of the rich man's

What Do We Do?

barns," Luke 12:15-21
When have you been greedy?

What Do We Do?

Jesus called all the parents and kids together and said, "Now pay attention to this—the T.V. shows you watch don't make you good or bad. It's what shows in your heart that matters."

"The proverb of what defiles a man," Matthew 15:10-12, 15-20; Mark 7:14-23

When have you broken a rule for a good reason?

What Do We Do?

Jesus' friends came to him and said, "Do you know that your stories are making the religious people angry?"

And Jesus said, "Every plant not planted by my Father in heaven will be pulled out of the garden. Leave them alone. They are blind, yet try to lead the blind. Can a blind adult lead a blind child? Won't they both fall into a ditch?"

"The proverb of every plant not planted," Matthew 15:13
"The proverb of the blind leading the blind," Matthew 15:14; Luke 6:39

How do you know whom to follow?

What Do We Do?

Watching how the kids all tried to be first in line, Jesus told them a story, "When you're picked for a baseball team don't go right to the pitcher's mound as if you're going to be the pitcher.

"If you do, the captain of the team might say, 'No, you're not good enough to be pitcher,' and might call someone else to take your place and you'll have to go out to right field feeling ashamed.

"Instead, when you're picked for a team, go right to the outfield. Then the captain might say, 'Hey, man, come in and pitch for us,' and you will come to the mound proudly.

"Everyone who cuts to the front of the line will be sent to the back. And everyone who goes to the back of the line will be brought up to the front."

"The parable of choosing the best seats," Luke 14 7-11

Have you ever been moved from the front of a line to the back? How did that feel?

What Do We Do?

Jesus told his friends, "If you're not ready to do hard things that might hurt, then you can't follow me.

"What kid when he starts to bake cookies doesn't look to make sure he has enough chocolate chips and sugar and flour to make a batch? Otherwise he'll get halfway and have to stop and his older brother will laugh and say, 'You couldn't finish what you started.'

"Or what coach doesn't count her players before a game to make sure she has enough to field a team. And if she doesn't, she'll quickly call the coach of the other team and postpone the game instead of having to forfeit."

"The parable of the tower," Luke 14:28-30
"The parable of the king making war," Luke 14:31-32

What hard things does Jesus ask you to do?

What Do We Do?

Jesus told his friends, "There was a rich father who gave his children big allowances. But one day he discovered that his oldest daughter had stolen money from his room. He called her in and said, 'Go get the money you've stolen and bring it to me. Then we have to talk.'

"As the daughter went to get the money she thought to herself, 'What am I going to do? Father will stop giving me my allowance for sure, and how will I get any spending money? I hate babysitting and I'm too ashamed to beg money from my friends. I know! I'll do something special for my brother and sister and then they'll have to help me out later.'

"So she got the money she'd stolen and went to her brother and said, 'Here's $30. Take it, no questions asked.' Then she went to her sister and said, 'Here's $20. Take it, no questions asked.'

"And her father praised her cleverness.

"Bad kids are more clever than good kids. Be clever in making heavenly friends."

"The parable of the unjust
steward," Luke 16:1-9

What Do We Do?

What have you done to make a heavenly friend?

What Do We Do?

Jesus asked his friends, "What if greedy, old Ebenezer Scrooge hadn't changed? The poor crippled boy, Tiny Tim, would have died because his father didn't earn enough money from Scrooge to pay for a doctor. Tiny Tim would have gone to heaven and there Father Christmas would have comforted him and made him happy. When Scrooge died he would have become a miserable ghost like his old partner Jacob Marley, wrapped in chains and misery. Looking up from hell to heaven, Scrooge would have seen Tiny Tim sitting happily on the lap of Father Christmas.

"Scrooge would have called out, 'Father Christmas help me. Send Tiny Tim to loosen my chains so that they don't hurt so much.'

"But Father Christmas would have answered, 'Child, remember the good things you had in life, and the bad things that Tim had. Now he is happy and you are suffering. Besides, there's a great cliff between you and us to keep us from crossing to you and to keep you from crossing to us.'

"Scrooge would have said, 'Then please send Tiny Tim back to Earth to warn other greedy people so they don't end up like me.'

What Do We Do?

"But Father Christmas would have answered, 'They have Moses, Elijah, Elisha, Isaiah, Jeremiah, Ezekiel, Daniel, Hosea, Joel, Amos, Obadiah, Jonah, Micah, Nahum, Habakkuk, Zephaniah, Haggai, Zechariah, and Malachi to listen to.'

"'No Father Christmas, they will surely listen to someone who comes back from the dead,' Scrooge would have said.

"But Father Christmas would have told Scrooge, 'If they don't listen to Moses, Elijah, Elisha, Isaiah, Jeremiah, Ezekiel, Daniel, Hosea, Joel, Amos, Obadiah, Jonah, Micah, Nahum, Habakkuk, Zephaniah, Haggai, Zechariah, and Malachi, they won't listen even to someone who comes back from the dead.'"

"The parable of Lazarus and the rich man," Luke 16:19-31

What have you done to help someone who was poor? What more could you do?

What Do We Do?

The children who were close to Jesus said to him, "Help us obey God more."

And Jesus answered, "If you were as obedient as a cat, you would have a golden halo shining over your head.

"Say you're a teacher and you tell your class that the Nile is the longest river in the world. Do you want your students to say, 'We believe you! We believe you!'?

"No. You want them to learn it because it's true. So when you have faith in God, say, 'We're not angels. We're just learning what's true.'"

"The parable of faith as a grain of mustard seed," Luke 17:5-6
"The parable of the servants' duty," Luke 17:7-10

Who do you know who obeys God a lot? What do they do?

What Do We Do?

Jesus told this story: "Two girls went to synagogue one Saturday. One of them was a good girl and the other was bad.

"The good girl liked to sit as close to the front as she could. During the service she prayed, 'God, thank you that I'm not like that bad girl. I do everything right.'

"But the bad girl stood in the back of the synagogue and wouldn't even look up at the rabbi. During the service that girl prayed, 'God, forgive me for all the bad things I've done.'

"I say that God came to the bad girl rather than to the good girl that day. Everyone who acts proud will be humbled, and everyone who acts humble will be made proud."

"The parable of the Pharisee and the tax-collector," Luke 18:9-14

Have you ever felt you were good? What did you do? Have you ever felt you were bad? What did you do?

What Do We Do?

"What do you think?" Jesus asked. "A father had two sons. He went to his first son and said, 'Please clean your room today.'

"And the son said, 'Sure.' But he didn't.

"The father went to his second son and said the same thing, 'Please clean your room today.'

"The second son said, 'I don't want to.' But later he changed his mind and cleaned his room.

"So which of the sons, do you think, obeyed his father?"

"The parable of the two sons," Matthew 21:28-32

Which son obeyed his father? Why?

What Do We Do?

Jesus said, "When God's Chosen One comes in power all of the schools will be gathered in front of him and he will separate them like a coach separates good players from bad players. He will put the good schools on his right side and the bad schools on his left.

"Then the Coach will say to those on his right side, 'You are winners in God's eyes. Come to the great party God's always planned for you because when I was new you welcomed me, when I was failing you taught me, when I was made fun of you defended me, when I was in trouble you helped me, when I was sick you visited me, and when I was lonely you made friends with me.'

"Then the good schools will ask him, 'Coach, when did we welcome you when you were new? When did we teach you when you were failing? When did we defend you when you were being made fun of? When did we help you when you were in trouble? When did we visit you when you were sick? When did we make friends with you when you were lonely?'

"And the Coach will say, 'What you did for the littlest kid you did for me.'

What Do We Do?

"Then the Coach will say to those on his left side, 'You are losers in God's eyes. Go off to the detention that God's planned for you because when I was new you didn't welcome me, when I was failing you didn't teach me, when I was made fun of you didn't defend me, when I was in trouble you didn't help me, when I was sick you didn't visit me, and when I was lonely you didn't make friends with me.'

"Then the bad schools will ask him, 'Coach, when didn't we welcome you when you were new? When didn't we teach you when you were failing? When didn't we defend you when you were being made fun of? When didn't we help you when you were in trouble? When didn't we visit you when you were sick? When didn't we make friends with you when you were lonely?'

"And the Coach will say, 'What you didn't do for the littlest kid you didn't do for me.' And the bad schools will all have detention, but the good schools will have a great party."

"The parable of the last judgment," Matthew 25:31-46

How well are we taking care of kids who are new, failing, being made fun of, in trouble, sick, and lonely? What more do we need to do?

What Do We Do?

    "Look and see how God's restaurant is full of people," Jesus said. "Already the waitresses and waiters are serving and getting heavenly tips. The cooks and the waitresses are celebrating. Some are cooks and some are waiters. I send you to serve what you haven't cooked. Others have cooked, and you are serving what they've made."

"The allegory of the fields ready to harvest," John 4:35-38

Have you ever felt filled with God? What helped you feel that way?

Who Is Jesus?

One day John the Baptist's friends came to Jesus and said, "We follow the rules and the other religious people follow the rules, so why don't your friends follow the rules?"

Jesus answered them, "When the guest has come it's not time to clean your house. But when the guest is taken away, then my friends will clean their homes as you do."

Then Jesus told them, "No one puts a new video game in an old type of player. It won't work and might even break it. Instead you need a new player for a new game.

"No one pours hot new pudding into a bowl of old pudding. If you do, the old pudding will melt and the new pudding will have big lumps. Instead you pour the new pudding into a clean new bowl. Then you have both the old and the new.

"And isn't it true that no kid wants to switch from a food she likes to a new food? Instead she says, 'What I already like is good enough for me.'"

"The parable of the groomsmen not fasting," Matthew 9:14-15; Mark 2:18-20; Luke 5:33-35
"The proverb of the new piece patching an old garment," Matthew 9:16; Mark 2:21; Luke 5:36
"The proverb of new wine in old wineskins," Matthew 9:17; Mark 2:22; Luke 5:37-38
"The proverb of old wine," Luke 5:39

What's new about Jesus?

Who Is Jesus?

The lawyers from the capital said, "Jesus is crazy. That's why he can cure crazy people."

But Jesus called them over to ask them some riddles. "Can craziness cure craziness? Can a cold make you well? If craziness cures craziness then it's not crazy. Before you can steal from the devil you have to tie him up."

"The parable of Satan casting out Satan," Matthew 12:24-29; Mark 3:22-27; Luke 11:15-22

What do these riddles mean?

Who Is Jesus?

"What's served at God's restaurant?" Jesus asked. "Bread from heaven. What is this heavenly bread? Me. I am the living bread from heaven. Eat this bread and you will live in heaven."

"The allegory of the living bread," John 6:50-58

How can bread live?

Who Is Jesus?

Jesus stood up in front of a crowd and said, "Are you thirsty? Then come to me and drink. Come to God's restaurant where we serve living water."

"The allegory of the living water,"
John 7:37-38

How can water live?

Who Is Jesus?

Jesus said, "The bad is like glue. When you do something bad it sticks to you. But you're not stuck forever. I am free forever. I can set you free from the bad. And if I set you free, you are really free."

"The allegory of the servant of sin," John 8:34-36

When have you been freed from something bad?

Who Is Jesus?

Jesus said, "I tell you the truth, the person who sneaks into the school through a back door or a window is a thief or a kidnapper.

"But the person who goes into the school through the front door is the teacher. The custodian opens the door for her. The students know her. She calls them by name and she teaches them. When her students go out to play, she leads them, and they follow her, because they know her.

"The students won't follow a stranger. Instead they'll run away, for they don't know the stranger."

"The parable of the sheepfold,"
John 10:1-6

Have you ever heard Jesus call you? When?

"Hear another story," Jesus said. "There was a woman who made a fine baseball diamond in her huge backyard. She had the ground flattened and bluegrass planted. She had the dirt base path smoothed and the bases tied down. But her job transferred her, so she and her family had to move far away. She told the neighborhood children they could use the field as much as they wanted as long as they took care of it.

"A few months later she told a friend that his children could play baseball there while they were visiting her old hometown. But the neighborhood kids chased her friend's children away and even threw rocks at them.

"When the woman heard about it she called another friend and asked her to go talk to the kids. But the neighborhood kids were rude and insulting and even threw rocks at her too.

"Last of all the woman sent her son all the way back to their hometown to talk to the kids. But when the kids saw her son they said to each other, 'If we chase him away then this baseball field will really be ours.' So they threw rocks at him until he was bleeding.

Who Is Jesus?

"When the woman comes back, what will she do to those children?"

> "The parable of the lord of the vineyard," Matthew 21:33-41; Mark 12:1-9; Luke 20:9-16
>
> *What will she do?*

Who Is Jesus?

Jesus said to them, "Haven't you read the story of Noah, how everybody laughed at him? But Noah listened and God came only to him and asked him to build the ark. And wasn't it great how God saved him and his family? I tell you, someone greater than Noah is here with you now.

"God won't come to you when you laugh at God. God will come instead to someone else who listens."

"The parable of the stone which the builders rejected," Matthew 21:42-44; Mark 12:10-11; Luke 20:17-18

Who do you know who listens to God? How do they do that?

Who Is Jesus?

Jesus said, "I tell you the truth, if the caterpillar doesn't bury itself in its cocoon it will never change. But if it does bury itself, then it will change into something brand new."

"The proverb of the grain of wheat," John 12:24

How did Jesus change?

Who Is Jesus?

Jesus said, "I am the true tree and my Father is the gardener. If a branch doesn't have fruit, then He cuts it off. If a branch does have fruit, then He cuts it back so it will have more fruit next year.

"Stay in me. And I will stay in you. The branch can't have fruit by itself; neither can you. You must stay part of the tree. I am the tree and you are the branches. If you stay in me you'll have a lot of fruit. But away from me you can do nothing."

"The allegory of the true vine,"
John 15:1-8

How do you stay in Jesus?

Who Is Jesus?

Jesus said, "When you run a race your legs hurt and your lungs ache. But when you cross the finish line you don't remember the pain.

"Soon you'll be sad because I'm leaving. But I will see you again. And then you'll be happy. That happiness no one can take away from you."

"The allegory of the woman giving birth," John 16:21-22

When you think about Jesus:
what makes you sad?
what makes you happy?

Postscript for Adults

How dare I recast Jesus' parables? With trepidation, but also with joy.

My trepidation is of course in touching and playing with what I believe is holy. For me, Jesus' parables, proverbs, and allegories are sacred text. So why dare to change them one tittle? Why take such liberties? Because I felt inspired to do so; because we are free to do so; because reshaping and retelling wisdom stories is an honored and powerful way to enter into their truth.

I had been thinking how to recast the parable of the pitiless slave so that my son could relate to it. There was an issue in his life that I knew this parable spoke to, but I also knew that he wouldn't see himself in the gospel text, that he might understand the point, but only in an abstract way, not in a way that would touch him at the moment with a message for his own life. Then I had an inspiration. I was given an idea, as writers get inspired ideas, appearing out of the blue, unpremeditated, uncalculated, which we attribute to the muse, to the spirit, to God, because we know that the idea is something truer than ourselves. I should write a book retelling Jesus' parables for children. I was excited. It was late, but I immediately wrote out two. The idea had all the hallmarks of a true inspiration—it energized me physically; it excited me mentally; it felt just right; it filled me with joy.

Christians are free to retell and interpret the Bible for their lives and their time. This we learned from our Jewish brethren and their rabbinical tradition of interpretation, disputation, and literary creation profoundly displayed in the Talmud. This is a significant teaching of the rabbinically trained Paul of Tarsus. In his letter to the Galatians the Apostle Paul declares, "For freedom Christ has set us free." Part of that freedom, Paul held, was the freedom to speak and write from our own experience mysteriously within "the mind of Christ." Paul balanced the importance of scripture with the vitality of God's spirit alive in the new community. He appealed to "the testimony of our conscience" as well as to the declarations of the Jewish prophets. He urged the young churches to not quench the spirit, to not despise contemporary prophesying, to "test everything," and to "hold fast to what is good." "The word is near you, on your lips and in your heart ...," Paul counseled the Roman church. To the Corinthians Paul recommended a practice of sharing their gifts: "When you come together, each one has a hymn, a lesson, a revelation, a tongue, or an interpretation. Let all things be done for edification." This role of interpretation and personal response was an essential issue for the Protestant reformers who argued that the individual believer was not simply bidden to accept the traditional reading of a received text, but must be free to struggle with the text to make it one's own. And this is the tradition of the original English novel—John Bunyan's allegorical masterpiece *Pilgrim's*

Progress—and all the allegories, stories, fancies, and retellings that have followed.

But Jesus used children as the model not the audience for his stories. Are his messages meant for children? It was the adults, he said, who had to change and follow the example of children. Wasn't his message to children simply two open arms and a blessing? Fundamentally yes, but it's also true that the human hunger for stories is perfected in children. What Reynolds Price has written in his book *A Palpable God* applies as equally to children as to adults: "We crave nothing less then perfect story; ... we are satisfied only by the one short tale we feel to be true: *History is the will of a just god who knows us.*"

Wisely or foolishly, Christians feel compelled to tell Jesus' stories to our children. The question is how we do it. We are constantly retelling and interpreting the Bible for children. And, unfortunately, we can do a poor job of it, especially in that often painful part of a Sunday service—the children's sermon—where our tendency is to simultaneously over-explain and obscure the issue. Our bad children's sermons are usually "parental stories," in Douglas Adams' terms, stories that are focused on saying the right things and delivering the party line. Adams warns in his book *The Prostitute in the Family Tree: Discovering Humor and Irony in the Bible* that "Parental stories are solemn and can kill by prescribing an ideal we cannot fulfill." "If Jesus' parables were parental stories," Adams writes, "they would concern such things as a perfect family, a perfect dinner party, a just manager, a just judge, a merciful slave, and a rich wise man." But they don't, do they? Jesus' parables are what Adams calls "grandparent stories," stories that aren't concerned about being right, but about being true, stories that "are humorous and give hope and life by sharing a reality similar to our own.... stories about a prodigal family, a busted banquet, an unjust manager, an unjust judge, an unmerciful slave, and a rich fool." I hope that my retellings retain some of Jesus' grandparent zest and that they might serve as more concrete and piquant children's sermons, stories that kids could act out, stories closer to the life kids know, stories that might even unsettle the parents sitting in the pews.

We interpret and retell wisdom stories because we know that in spite of the inadequacy of our attempts, in spite of the adulterations we intentionally and unintentionally introduce, the act of retelling is a time-proven way of opening our eyes to the truth. The retelling can release for us the power in the word; it can be milk preparing us for the scripture's meat. And I think this is especially true with Jesus' stories because they are so often similes or metaphors pointing to spiritual realities beyond us. The spiritual truths that Jesus wants to teach just can't be learnt propositionally or philosophically. They must be understood by the spirit more than the mind. The mind actually gets in the way of understanding as much as attitudes or habits.

Parables, proverbs, allegories, all encompassed in the Hebrew word "mashal," were the rabbinical answer to the conundrum of having to use words to describe a spiritual realm that is beyond our words. A mashal is the Jewish equivalent of a Zen koan, a puzzle that is only understood as it's unpacked and responded to. Mashals and koans are designed to break through a listener's comfortable perspective in order to reveal a new way of understanding our lives, the world, and the spirit. This understanding uncovered within a mashal is called in Hebrew the "nimshal." Unlike a dogmatic assertion, a koan or mashal does not lend itself to philosophical dissection. You cannot understand one without internalizing that understanding, without having its nimshal unfold within you. To understand them is to change your way of thinking. Listeners who are resistant to that change will not understand; they will have ears and not hear, eyes and not see.

Jesus is incessantly tossing out similes for the kingdom of God to his disciples—"It is like this, it is like that...." He could go on forever because the various parables were but signs pointing to one great, numinous, shocking, and comforting reality. The next example he came up with might just be the one that allowed the kingdom to break in on their hearts.

The one obvious way of misinterpreting the parables is to take them literally. But to grapple with them imaginatively, to ask, "If the kingdom of God is like leaven is it also like a joke?" has been for me a way to stretch my mind and become more permeable to their light. With these retellings I hope to surprise children and point them to the mysterious and upside-down nature of the kingdom Jesus is inaugurating. I want them to puzzle through contemporary versions of Jesus' puzzles, and in puzzling to have God's spirit open their minds about who He is and who He can be for them.

How dare I recast Jesus' stories? With joy. It has been joy to sit with these holy stories, to meditate on them, to play with them, and to try to let their power course through me.

Postscript for Adults

I have added questions to each of my retellings under the encouragement of my friend Dr. Rob Johnson so that the reader or listener may "stop and consider what the parable means—in general and for their life specifically." "That's a principle of learning theory that I find increasingly important," Rob explained, "Unless we're either encouraged or forced to stop and re-frame the lesson in our own language and through the prism of our own life experience, little sustained learning occurs. That's true neuro-biologically also, in terms of how new memories are made and learning occurs."

By my count Jesus tells 78 unique stories in the gospels. In that number I'm including his parables, proverbs, and allegories. In those stories Jesus explores three major themes:

1. The kingdom of God (32 stories)
2. Our response to God's kingdom (32 stories)
3. His role in that kingdom (14 stories)

As the Venn diagram below shows, 13 of Jesus' stories appear in all three synoptic gospels (Matthew, Mark and Luke). In keeping with its distinctiveness the gospel of John shares none of its nine stories with the other gospels, and its stories are primarily focused on Jesus' role and identity. John's gospel does not even use the same Greek word to describe the stories; it uses the Greek word "paroimia," which is often translated into English as "allegory," but may also be translated as "proverb" (See John 16:25, 29). The synoptic gospels, on the other hand, use the Greek word "parabole," which is consistently translated into English as "parable." Matthew and Luke share 15 additional stories between them.

Postscript for Adults

Matthew and Mark share 2 additional stories. Luke and Mark share 1 additional story. Mark has 2 unique stories, Matthew has 13, and Luke has 23.

Venn Diagram Showing How Jesus's Parables are Shared across the Four Gospels

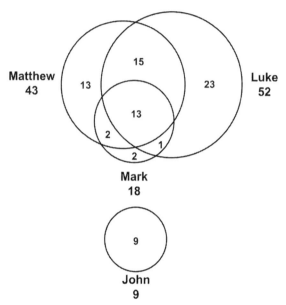

Parable, Proverb, or Allegory	Unique	Matthew	Mark	Luke	John
Totals	78	43	18	52	9

The following table shows the gospel references for each of the 78 stories, the thematic section I've included each in, and the page number where you can find them. The parables, proverbs, and allegories are sorted by the number of their appearances in the gospels, with the 13 that appear in all three Synoptic Gospels listed first.

Postscript for Adults

Thematic Section	#	Parable, Proverb, Allegory	Matthew	Mark	Luke	John	Page #
What Do We Do?	1	Salt	5:13	9:50	14:34-35		*53*
What Do We Do?	2	The lamp under the bushel	5:14-16	4:21-22	8:16; 11:33		*45*
Who is Jesus?	3	The groomsmen not fasting	9:14-15	2:18-20	5:33-35		*75*
Who is Jesus?	4	The new piece patching an old garment	9:16	2:21	5:36		*75*
Who is Jesus?	5	New wine in old wineskins	9:17	2:22	5:37-38		*75*
Who is Jesus?	6	Satan casting out Satan	12:24-29	3:22-27	11:15-22		*77*
How Does God Come To Us?	7	The sower	13:3-8	4:3-8	8:4-8		*1*
How Does God Come To Us?	8	The grain of mustard seed	13:31-32	4:30-32	13:18-19		*13*
How Does God Come To Us?	9	The children	18:2-4; 19:13-15	10:13-16	18:15-17		*22*
How Does God Come To Us?	10	The camel through the eye of the needle	19:23-26	10:23-27	18:24-27		*23*
Who is Jesus?	11	The lord of the vineyard	21:33-41	12:1-9	20:9-16		*82*
Who is Jesus?	12	The stone which the builders rejected	21:42-44	12:10-11	20:17-18		*84*
How Does God Come to Us?	13	The fig tree's tender branches	24:32-33	13:28-29	21:30-31		*31*

Postscript for Adults

Thematic Section	#	Parable, Proverb, Allegory	Matthew	Mark	Luke	John	Page #
What Do We Do?	14	What defiles a man	15:10-12, 15-20	7:14-23			61
What Do We Do?	15	The hand that offends	18:8-9	9:43-48			52
What Do We Do?	16	Going before the judge	5:25-26		12:58-59		54
What Do We Do?	17	The eye as the lamp of the body	6:22-23		11:34-36		48
What Do We Do?	18	The mote in your brother's eye, the beam in your own	7:3-5		6:41-42		46
What Do We Do?	19	The son asking for bread	7:9-11		11:11-13		49
How Does God Come To Us?	20	The narrow door	7:13-14		13:23-24		7
What Do We Do?	21	The good tree and the bad	7:16-20		6:43-44		47
What Do We Do?	22	Building on rock or sand	7:24-27		6:47-49		50
How Does God Come To Us?	23	The plentiful harvest	9:37-38		10:2		12
What Do We Do?	24	The return of the unclean spirit	12:43-45		11:24-26		58
How Does God Come To Us?	25	The leaven	13:33		13:20-21		14
What Do We Do?	26	The blind leading the blind	15:14		6:39		62
How Does God Come To Us?	27	The lost sheep	18:12-14		15:3-7		19

Postscript for Adults

Thematic Section	#	Parable, Proverb, Allegory	Matthew	Mark	Luke	John	Page #
How Does God Come To Us?	28	The housemaster knowing the hour of the thief	24:42-44		12:39-40		28
How Does God Come To Us?	29	The wise and evil servants	24:45-51		12:42-48		30
How Does God Come To Us?	30	The talents	25:14-30		19:11-27		41
How Does God Come To Us?	31	The watching servants		13:34-36	12:35-38		28
What Do We Do?	32	Wolves in sheep's clothing	7:15				47
How Does God Come To Us?	33	The wheat and tares	13:24-30				4
How Does God Come To Us?	34	The treasure in the field	13:44				15
How Does God Come To Us?	35	The pearl of great price	13:45-46				16
How Does God Come To Us?	36	The net cast into the sea	13:47-50				17
How Does God Come To Us?	37	The scribe who becomes a disciple	13:52				18
What Do We Do?	38	Every plant not planted	15:13				62
How Does God Come To Us?	39	The pitiless slave	18:23-35				20

Postscript for Adults

Thematic Section	#	Parable, Proverb, Allegory	Matthew	Mark	Luke	John	Page #
How Does God Come To Us?	40	The generous lord of the vineyard	20:1-16				24
What Do We Do?	41	The two sons	21:28-32				71
How Does God Come To Us?	42	The prince's marriage	22:1-14				26
How Does God Come To Us?	43	The wise and foolish virgins	25:1-13				39
What Do We Do?	44	The last judgment	25:31-46				72
How Does God Come To Us?	45	The seed cast on the earth		4:26-29			3
What Do We Do?	46	Being salted with fire		9:49			52
Who is Jesus?	47	Old wine			5:39		75
What Do We Do?	48	Treasure of the heart			6:45		47
How Does God Come To Us?	49	Children sitting in the marketplace			7:31-35		10
What Do We Do?	50	A certain creditor			7:40-43		51
How Does God Come To Us?	51	The hand to the plough			9:62		11
What Do We Do?	52	The good Samaritan			10:25-37		55
What Do We Do?	53	The friend at midnight			11:5-8		57
What Do We Do?	54	The rich man's barns			12:15-21		59
How Does God Come To Us?	55	The fig tree without fruit			13:6-9		29

Postscript for Adults

Thematic Section	#	Parable, Proverb, Allegory	Matthew	Mark	Luke	John	Page #
How Does God Come To Us?	56	The housemaster shutting the door			13:25-27		8
How Does God Come To Us?	57	The last that shall be first			13:28-30		9
What Do We Do?	58	Choosing the best seats			14:7-11		63
How Does God Come To Us?	59	The great supper			14:15-24		32
What Do We Do?	60	The tower			14:28-30		64
What Do We Do?	61	The king making war			14:31-32		64
How Does God Come To Us?	62	The lost drachma			15:8-10		34
How Does God Come To Us?	63	The prodigal son			15:11-32		35
What Do We Do?	64	The unjust steward			16:1-9		65
What Do We Do?	65	Lazarus and the rich man			16:19-31		67
What Do We Do?	66	Faith as a grain of mustard seed			17:5-6		69
What Do We Do?	67	The servants' duty			17:7-10		69
How Does God Come To Us?	68	The judge who didn't fear God			18:1-8		38
What Do We Do?	69	The Pharisee and the tax-collector			18:9-14		70
How Does God Come To Us?	70	Being born of the spirit				3:3-8	6

100

Postscript for Adults

Thematic Section	#	Parable, Proverb, Allegory	Matthew	Mark	Luke	John	Page #
What Do We Do?	71	The fields ready to harvest				4:35-38	74
Who is Jesus?	72	The living bread				6:50-58	78
Who is Jesus?	73	The living water				7:37-38	79
Who is Jesus?	74	The servant of sin				8:34-36	80
Who is Jesus?	75	The sheepfold				10:1-6	81
Who is Jesus?	76	The grain of wheat				12:24	85
Who is Jesus?	77	The true vine				15:1-8	86
Who is Jesus?	78	The woman giving birth				16:21-22	87

Index

Index

Index

Kent Chadwick is a poet living on Bainbridge Island, Washington. His poetry CD, *Still through you* was recorded at Jack Straw Productions in 2003. His poetry-painting collaborations with his brother Gregg Chadwick include the installation "Poets + Painters" at the di Rosa Preserve Gallery in Napa Valley, California and Burning Man, both in 2003. Their collaborations are documented on their website Ars Poetica: http://chadwick15.home.mindspring.com/.

Made in the USA
Charleston, SC
06 October 2010